SUNDAY the 13th

Stephen Gard

illustrated by Gary Anderson

GINN

Contents

Chapter One

About Bugley

They keep asking me where Bugley is. I keep telling them I don't know. He sat next to me before lunchtime and then he went out to lunch. Then he went to the library. Now no-one can find him. And Lisa has gone, too.

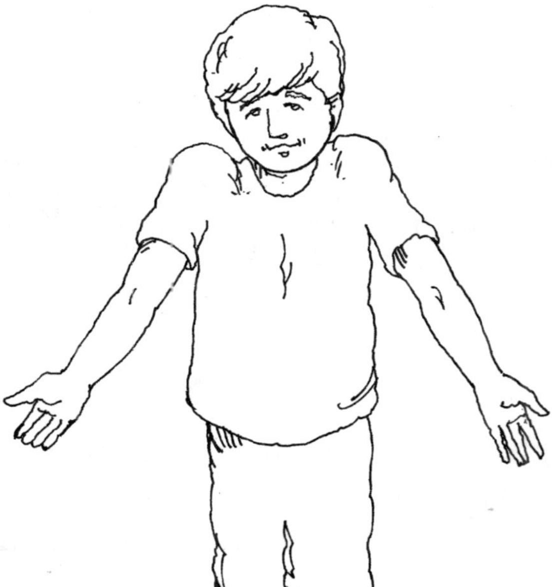

Bugley is my best mate. Bugley is small and he wears these big glasses, so he looks like he has bug-eyes. And he's always doing science stuff.

He mixes up gunk. He joins up wires. He traps bugs in a bug-trapper, and catches tadpoles in jars. So we call him Bugley.

If Bugley gets something for a birthday or Christmas, he takes it to bits right away. Then he spends ages putting it back together again. Sometimes it works again, but mostly it doesn't.

You should see Bugley's bedroom. It's full of junk. If you want to visit Bugley's room, you have to climb in the window. He goes down to the dump and gets old radios and bits of bike. He picks up pipes and taps and wires and stuffs them in his schoolbag.

When he gets home, his mum looks in his bag, and she says, "No way, Bradley!" That's his real name, Bradley. And his mum chucks all the junk in the bin. Bugley looks at her sadly with his big, bug-eyes, and later he climbs out the window and gets it all back.

Once Bugley made a Homework Machine out of junk. It looked like a letterbox with a light on top. All you did was put your homework book in it. The light went on, and the next morning you took it out, and the homework was done. But it didn't work. It cooked Bugley's homework book instead.

So . . . here I am, sitting outside the office at school. While I'm waiting, I'll tell you a bit more about me and Bugley and Lisa. And then you can work out where they went, because I don't know. Anyway, I don't think I know.

Chapter Two

Bugley's birthday

One day Bugley came to school and gave out some cards that said "Please come to my birthday party". The party was on Sunday the 13th. Bugley was going to be twelve, so his mum said he could have twelve kids at his party.

“Where’s my card?” said Lisa. Lisa is the school’s handball killer. She also thinks that Bugley is nuts, but she wanted to go to his party.

“I can only ask twelve people,” said Bugley. “Sorry, Lisa.”

“Bugley,” said Lisa. “I want to go to your party.” She went right up close to him, and looked down into his big bug-eyes. “Please,” said Lisa.

So, thirteen kids went to the party. Well, it wasn't really a party because we went out all day. First, Bugley's mum and dad took us to the Science Show. Then we had lunch at the Chicken King.

Next, we went to Mega Land and played the pinnies and had rides on things that made us puke. We had takeaway for tea, and then we went to the pictures and saw *Subways of Blood*.

It was the best birthday ever.

Chapter Three

Bugley's video

Bugley's dad has this new video camera, and he took a video of everything we did on Bugley's birthday, even Bugley brushing his teeth in the morning.

Every day after school, Bugley watched his birthday video, over and over. Bugley loved it, and I used to crack up laughing. But when it was over, Bugley always looked a bit sad.

"That was the best day of my life," he said. "I wish I could do it all again."

"Wait till next birthday," I said. "We can go back."

"No," said Bugley. "It will never be the same."

Bugley pressed the rewind button on his video. He looked at me sadly with his big bug-eyes.

"I wish I could go back in Time," he said.

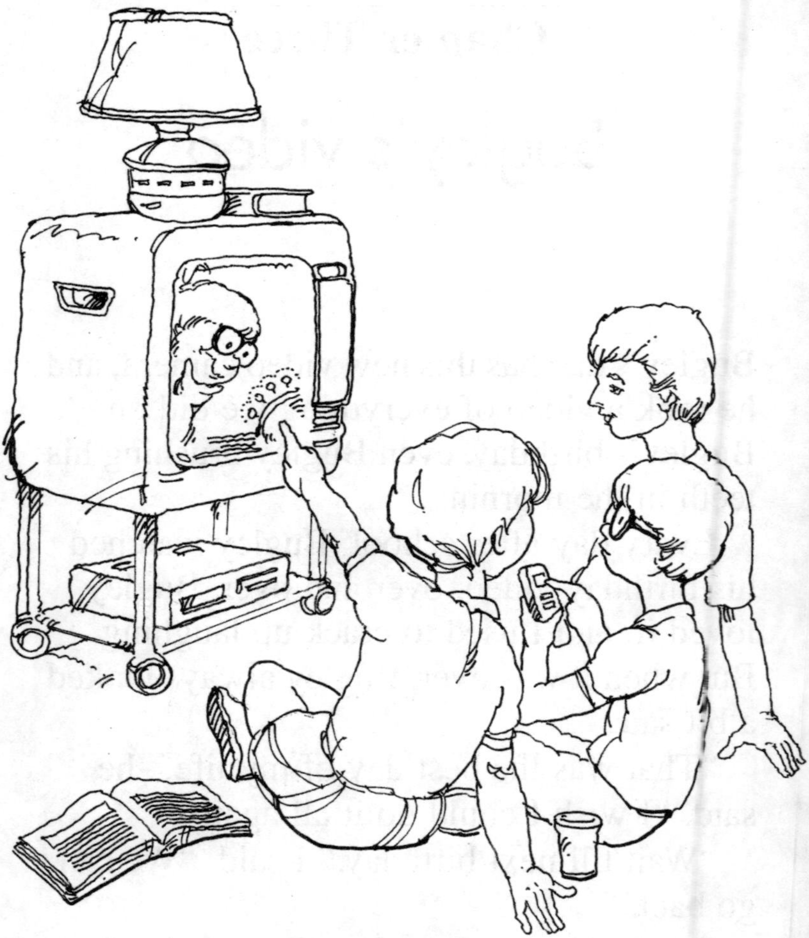

Next afternoon, we watched the video again. Lisa was with us. She kept telling Bugley to stop the video.

"I want to see that bit again," she laughed.

Bugley pressed the rewind button.

"There!" shouted Lisa.

Bugley pressed the pause button. There was Bugley, at the Science Show. He was making a funny face.

"I was looking at a really interesting machine," said Bugley.

"You look like a dag," said Lisa. "Now go fast forward. I want to see you on the Big Zipper again. When you sicked up."

But Bugley stared at the screen. The picture was stopped on his face.

"You see?" he said. "You can stop Time."

"What?" said Lisa.

"My birthday is still there," said Bugley. "I wish I could go back to it. Sunday the 13th. It was great."

Lisa laughed.

"You're nuts, Bugley. That's just a picture."

Bugley shook his head.

"Yesterday is still there. Time is like a video. You can rewind it. You can do it all again."

"How?" asked Lisa.

Bugley shook his head.

"I don't know," he said, "but I'll find out."

Chapter Four

Bugley's secret

The next day Bugley wasn't at school. He wasn't at school the day after, either. But he came back on Friday.

"Have you been sick?" I asked.

Bugley shook his head.

"I went somewhere," he said.

Lisa ran up to us.

"Who wants to be killed at handball?" she asked.

So we played handball. And Lisa killed us.

We talked about going to high school next year.

"You can do Science at high school," I said. "You can mix up gunk and join wires and cut up rats."

"I know," said Bugley. "But I'm scared of going to high school. I'm scared of the big kids."

"My mum is sending me away to boarding school," said Lisa. "No way. I'm not going."

"Where will you go?" I asked.

"I don't know," said Lisa. "I'll run away."

Now things started to get strange. Bugley was never around on the weekend, and he was away from school a lot. And he didn't bring any notes. Then one day Mr Clark said, "Bradley, come here, please."

Bugley went out the front to Mr Clark.

"Here's a note to your mum," said Mr Clark. "I would like to see her, please."

Bugley looked sadly at Mr Clark with his big, bug-eyes.

"Yes, sir," he said.

At playtime, Lisa and I asked Bugley what was going on.

"Where have you been?" I asked.

"How come you don't have any notes for being away?" asked Lisa.

"Sshh!" said Bugley. "Someone could hear us. Come over here."

Bugley led us over to some seats, away from everyone else.

"I found out how to do it," said Bugley. "I found out how to rewind Time. I keep going back to Sunday the 13th. It was the best day of my life."

Lisa said that Bugley was nuts. Bugley shook his head.

"Would you like to try it?" he asked.

Lisa laughed. Bugley got his bag. He took out the video of his birthday party on Sunday the 13th.

Then he took out something else, something made out of junk. It looked like a letterbox with a light on top.

"Bugley," I said, "that's your Homework Machine. And it doesn't even work."

Bugley looked at me with his big bug-eyes.

"I changed it," he said. "Now it's a Time Shifter. Let's go to the library."

We went into the library, and Bugley got out a book. He opened it, and showed us a picture of a brain.

"Kids have a Time Bump in their heads," he said. "It's a part of the brain, and we can learn to use it if we try. The Time Bump goes away when we grow up. But I know how to use it."

Then Bugley went to Mrs Ross, the teacher in charge of the library. He asked her if we could watch a video and she said "yes".

Bugley put his birthday video in the machine. He pressed the fast forward button until he saw the picture of his face, and then he pressed the pause button.

"Watch this," he said.

Bugley sat down very close to the screen and stared at the picture of his face. Then he put the Time Shifter on his head, like a hat. The light went on.

"Bugley!" I said. "Remember what happened to your homework book?"

"You're nuts, Bugley," said Lisa.

"Bugley!" I said. "Don't! You'll cook your head!"

“Sunday the 13th!” said Bugley.

And Bugley was gone. The Time Shifter was still there, but the light was out.

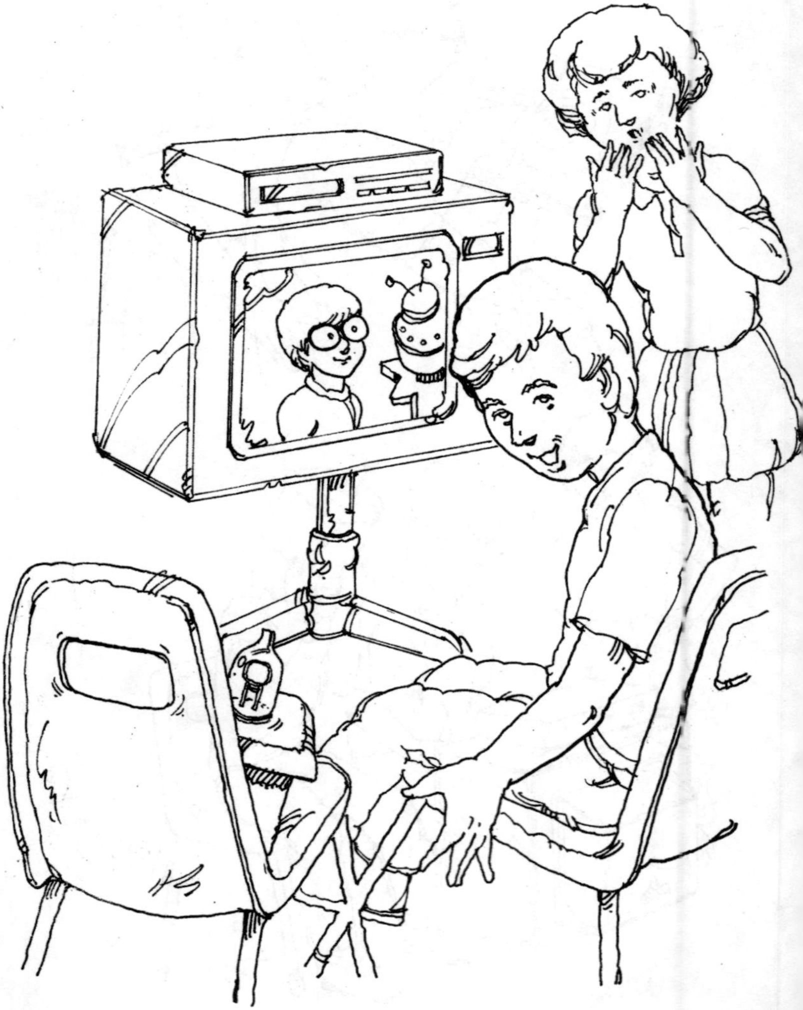

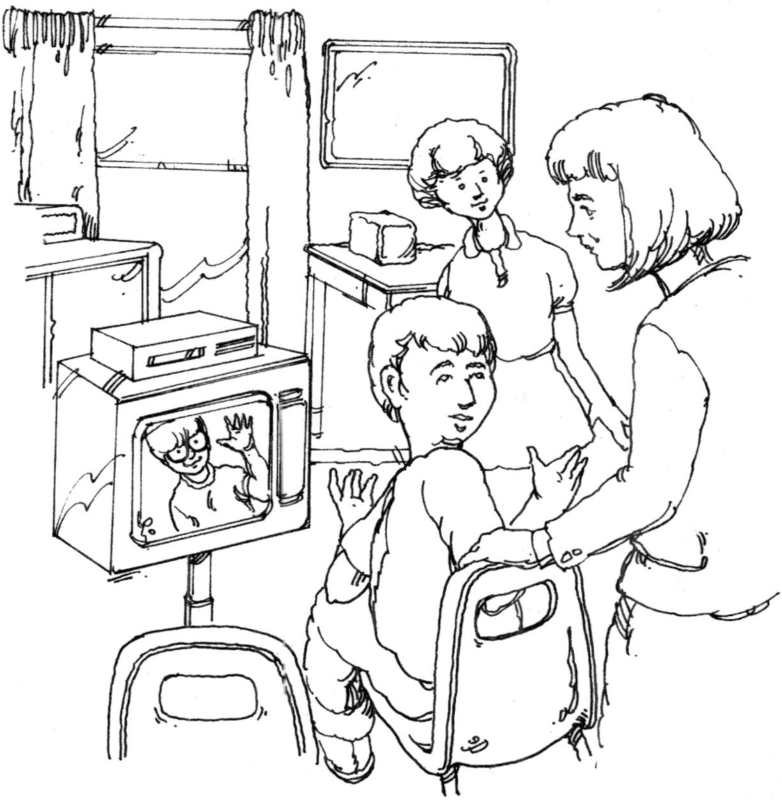

Lisa and I stared at the screen. Lisa didn't laugh. The video started to play again. There was Bugley at the Science Show. He was looking at an interesting machine. Then he turned around. He waved at us. "Hi Mrs Ross!" he called.

Lisa and I looked around. Mrs Ross was standing behind us.

"Where's Bradley?" she said. "Playtime is over. Turn off the video and go to lines, please."

She walked away.

"You see?" said Bugley.

We turned around. Bugley was back again. He took the video out, and picked up the Homework Machine.

"I want to try," said Lisa.

"Okay," said Bugley. "We'll come back at lunchtime."

Chapter Five

Where's Bugley?

But I got kept in at lunchtime. When I got out to the playground Lisa and Bugley weren't there. So I ran to the library. I couldn't see them, but Bugley's video was playing. I sat down and watched. There was Bugley, and there was Lisa — at the Science Show. They both turned around and waved to me.

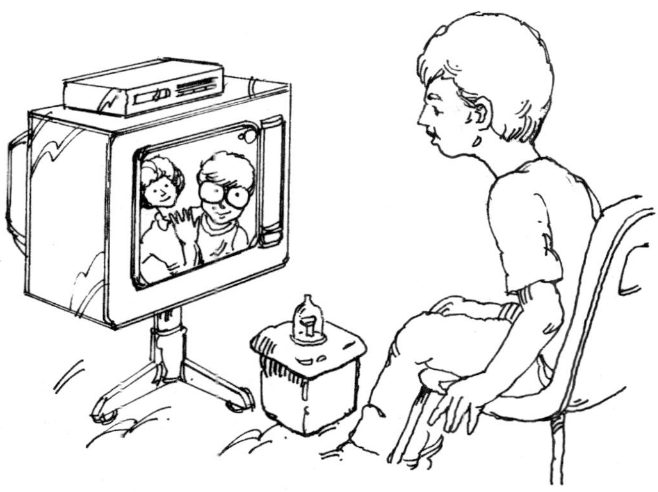

"Come on!" they called. "Come with us! Put on the Time Shifter!"

Just then, Mrs Ross came into the library.

"The bell will go soon," she said. "Please come back and watch that video later."

So I went out to lines. It was sports day, and Mr Clark called out names. Bugley didn't answer, and Lisa didn't answer. I started to feel really bad.

"Bradley! Lisa! Where are they?" asked Mr Clark. He looked straight at me. "Do you know?"

I looked at him for a long time, and then I shook my head.

"Did they jig it?" asked Mr Clark.

"I don't know, sir," I said.

"I think you do know," said Mr Clark. "Don't you?"

I looked at Mr Clark again for a long time. Then I nodded.

"Yes," said Mr Clark. "Please go to the office. I'll be along to talk to you there soon."

So here I am, sitting at the office. And something else is wrong.

Mrs Ross just came up to me.

"Is this your video? You left it in the library," she said.

"No," I said. "It's Bugley's. I mean, it's Bradley's."

"Oh," said Mrs Ross. "Well, will you please tell Bradley that I'm sorry."

She gave me the video.

"Thanks Mrs Ross," I said. "But why are you sorry?"

"Well," said Mrs Ross, "I forgot that Bradley's video was in the machine."

"Yes, Miss," I said.

"And I wiped it," said Mrs Ross. "I put a new TV show on Bradley's video. Sorry."

So I'm sitting at the office. Mr Clark will be here soon, and he's going to ask me where Bugley is. He'll ask me if I know where Lisa is. What am I going to tell him?

What would *you* tell him?